# Snow Drifts

Deven Philbrick

SPUYTEN DUYVIL

*New York City*

## Acknowledgements

The following poems have previously appeared in literary magazines.

"Space is the Place" – *Diode Poetry*

"Midnight in California" – *Protean Magazine*

"The We We'd Be" – *Night Music Journal*

"Character" – *Palooka*

"Trying to Tell the Story" – *Palooka*

"The Real Thing" – *Palooka*

"Self-Portrait" – *Palooka*

"Deep Listening" – *Obsidian*

"Stone" – *Zone 3*

ISBN 978-1-959556-10-7

*For Nathaniel Mackey and Will Alexander,*
*whose visionary works taught me how to write this book.*

*For Caroline Fernelius, whose love is everything.*

## SPACE IS THE PLACE

*Space is the place*
I've heard it said
or sung, the Sun
of our dreams not
returning, the never
of never said coming
back, black Sun, I've
heard them say, we
dreamt it another way,
cracked LP on a dirty
turntable, table turned
on the Sun, black like
a (k)night of a different
ordered pair, numerically
black sky speckled with
uncountable stars, black
fugitive, rot, not the space
of the exterior, the outer
layer of experience, the ex
of expression pumping out
black ink from squid corpse,
no, the space of the silent
h in heart, bad Babylon banging
down the door to the interior,
locked with a black key, where
I and I find what they said
would be there, but it's
unrecognizable, since it's too
black to see, *One Love* in black
ink, staining the sinew and tissue

rendered invisible by shadow
cast back, to be taken aback
by one's own shadow
is to see color for the first time
and remember the other Time,
the First Time, in whose shadow
we live our experiences,
daily and otherwise,
transcendent and otherwise,
mystical and otherunwise to that
beautiful shadowland, whatever
it is we trying to get back to.
And I hear it again.
*Space is the place*
I've come back from.
Having gone somewhere,
I release myself from that
wretched constellation in whose
grasp we've found ourselves
again and again and again.

## Midnight in California

It is midnight in California
        but it is three o'clock
in my refrigerator.
I have never been to California.
It is midnight in Nancy
Pelosi's claw-footed bathtub.
My pickles are ready for
bed.

With the exception of
            poetry
      California
has no
culture. It is three o'clock
in American culture.
It was three o'clock when
the settlers
         came.

It hasn't been three o'clock
in California in over a
        year.
This is the place-
        mat on which I spilled
pickle juice at one minute of two.
Yesterday, in California.
I am in California.

Today, there was baking
soda inside of my refrigerator.
Inside of California,
the forests are on fire today.
     I sold my refrigerator
     and my
           soul
to a South Korean diplomat for
      twenty-two-trillion pennies
but because of a loophole in our contract
I only received three dollars and fifty cents,
which I then used to purchase the pickles
that are scattered around my kitchen floor.
Californians don't eat pickles
     like I do.
The poem is not about California.
It is a blueprint for fissure—
yesterday, in California,
today where *I* am, an explosion
took place and rendered all within
its vicinity dead
     simultaneously.
My refrigerator is on fire.
It is three o'clock and I must clock
out
     of power
inside of California,
     inside of labor,
     inside of my bought and sold
           soul
like pickles dropped on the floor
     all at once.

THEREFORE—

I stare the stone in the face and it
       laughs at me, my awkward
       shape, my all too human tongue
and as I listen to its laughter, I feel ashamed
that my skeleton is inside of my skin.

The capacity I have for I
       is the capacity of the pronoun itself—
interiority is only an *experience* of inwardness—
asides aside, the stone shapes me as I
       shape it. I live for
       inwardness
but not evaluatively—to cultivate the resources of the human
imagination, I produce I. I produces I.

abstractions aside.

       Outside the dirty window, the sky is all awash in dark clouds.
       Inside, food is being eaten, coffee being drunk—the Muse's nest

Whose skeleton? Whose skin? I ask these questions plainly and without ulteriority.
       Ulteriority is poetry, an angel told me in a dream
              (a dream of light and limousine,
                     of Ronald Reagan in a gulag)

The sun has set on
imagination but
only as

        a concept.

After a long journey, I will have carried
       the stone into the sea.

## CHARACTER

*Symbol marked or branded on the body*

The character
of the memory
is such that if
one remembers
it correctly it
doesn't have
characters—

    Characteristics of remembering,
    discovering, the scene through
    the window on that snow
    bedusted evening—

The memory is a coming to character.

*Alphabetic letter, graphic symbol standing for a sound or syllable*

The door swung open loudly
and the man proclaimed: "not speech, but snow."

The child at the table coloring
a picture of a sunset on a beach
could hear the man identify the sketch
    as of a haystack.

*Symbol or imprint on the soul*

"Interpretation," a woman later insisted, "is
what allows me to see the picture one way
and you to see it another." The child doesn't
think of that woman as

                              a character


*A defining quality, individual feature*

Even a scream is an
            interpretive gesture,
the memory's meaning traveling
with its sound,
toward that unbearable tear in the seam of the scene
where what is seen and what is heard are
incongruous—the memory is
                  of a shining, bright-eyed face,
                  but the scream threatens
                  like a siren.


*Sum of qualities that define a person or thing and distinguish it from another*

Someone has crossed the lines
and the snow, now, outside
the window obscures the edges
of that psychic field of vision
into which the rememberer
                  looks.

*Person in a play or novel*

There are no characters
       in this memory,
only shadows shifting,
black, black, black,
against the snowy white
       night.

## THE WE WE'D BE

Speaking slant to historical
       tensions,
therein lies the occasional
demand. Occasion by time not
special,  tension by surface not
tense, tensed our thighs as we walked
the walk, the squawk of the walking
we'd do deafened us, deafening blast
we'd thought we'd heard, but hearing,
       lost word to Time,
never came
       as demanded. It's
a question of
       tense.
It(')s history, baby, and we know too
much to say, too much to touch, too
much to *speak slant*, as they say, the they
they knew they'd one day be, the being
they'd be thrown into, the seed sown
only for them. Birth, death and the other
thing, the quick surprise one reads about,
an amulet n all that, fundamental texture
of elemental torpor, essential switch
       of the withering
       spine,
it's fine, we swear it, our
lines never lie, the world lies,
lies in wait, telling its violent prevarications,

ennobling those of our mortal station
to puncture it with nimble barbs
      and ruinous imaginations.
*We thunder'd there*, we said
in our final dream, not collective but
      communal.
Careening and careering from one pole
to the next, death's a drift
      nearly continental,
      slow
      aching
      rapturous.

## DEEP LISTENING

*The classroom has its purpose*
said the angel to the toad
                    overheard
overstanding of sublinguistic
                    speech
the question of hearing
ringing in one's
            ears
years of arrears one pays
            to one's first time
listening
            after a long stretch
of unsolicited silence
in birth and
            prelinguistic childhood.


*Slip along the listening*
we heard the elders shout
                    down
the rapid count of
            telling it slant
the it itself not repeating
the hearing always already
            overheard
overlooked in the looking
            glass looked over

by fugitive onlookers
        overlookers
        overseers
mind over matter over
        overmind under
        oversoul
undersitting under the undertree
sprouting ear shaped fruit
        in the mind's ear.

*Youth you said*
you said burning like
        as or in
the Fire itself the fire
of chemical conditions and
        alchemical procedures
the already ready though all too
        true relation of *tous* to
        you me and three
the only thing there is
beyond overheard
echoes of long dead voices
screams made audible nevertheless
unheard.

Over and over we listen to the it
we dare not name
for fear it trap us under

the permanence of its
burning
    the heaviness
    the choke
and underground
we ground ourselves
screaming and chanting to great offense
and keep ourselves awake.

## JOHN CAGE (DIED INSIDE MY MIND)

The ringing of uninvited piano
invades, indeterminate bounce
determined by its spectral set.
Doors close and re-open. Drinks
clatter on unobtrusive trays. Stays
with you, the sound, the splay, the aural
darkness and its analog in mind.

White mind, I've heard it called. Walls
built with alien bricks, thick and sturdy,
washed by worn and weary hands, dirty
walls unacceptable in the face
of the never asked for piano. Face the sound,
face the mind, face determination, but do
no listening. Clockface belies time bought
and borrowed, reveals a rift riven
in ancient origin. I have no more time
for this soullessness, but there's nothing
to do but wait. Soul the missing link
between ascension and happening.

I don't know why I've come here.
Concentration's finite stores
abhor the conditions created by this
noise, indeterminate but not free, determined
by received meanings all the same. Someone's
coming to wash the walls, which get dirtier
with each shift of the clockface's spindly

hands and each random rumble of piano
sound, music only ostensibly. Melody
is meaningless. Build power. They serve
drinks here, but I won't partake. Poison
cup replaced sacred smoke. Joke silence caged.

Note for note, I know this one, played it
before in a dream. Heard the line in my
head before I played, performance's pulse
invading my prostrate corporeal husk, husk
worth sloughing to dream of sound. I know
the algorithm that got us here, no more
free than its institutional opposite, soul
slipping through cracks in the wall of sound,
humble in the face of it, dreaming of previously
unheard sonic mixes. Truth will set the music
free, determined not even by mind, white
or otherwise. Mind's power is deeper than that.
I wake in the old room, piano sounds
persisting all the same. Listening, now,
the lone holder of free meaning, afforded
without material cost, afforded without
determination. The door bursts open, pushed
perhaps by me. I flee, I flee, I don't look back,
and when I reach my place of rest, I'll hear it for real.

## WAKE

Adapted under certain
      conditions, conditions of
stress no less, distress what pain's
made out of, pain what makes up
dust, the kind we fly by, duress
what dust made dream. I'm not talking
about that kind of pain. The angle
of incision, protracted whip of endless
motion, is what determines the pain
of the cut, depth notwithstanding, dust
erased by bone, thrust up from spore, spun
out of the merely physical, pushed presence
of absence's pulse, induced breath and strain
and thus became. I am not a victim of this
infinite motion machine, but resting between
the surfaces of my body, I've mixed
everything I can
      because mixing
      is all there is
      to be done.
Fluids cannot be unstirred.
It is my condition
      and its qualities, like flies
swarming an elephant's soiled tail,
affix themselves to me via
the bodily gateway, passing thru the opening,
a reverse birth worth the breath
spent on breakfast or, even, on opening
my eyes just after sleeping, on only that briefest

moment during which I don't know
where I am, and the sand
in my pockets empties, fills the bed,
and I dream
       of being poured out of a bucket
       and the final grains
land far away from the initial heap. Soul
spent on dreaming
       under certain conditions, I've found
myself pouring inefficient contents
       into one collateral cup
and for those who drink from it,
       I don't know who,
it may make sense.
Dipping my foot in the bucket,
I rise from sleep, force the conditions
and stand. Under these, it happens
and shows no signs of stopping.

# Unless

1

Toast pops
         like
two or three minutes
before the coffee
is done.
It drips
         as
I retrieve a cup from
the cupboard.

A chip is
in the cup.
It could cut
my lip
         unless
I'm careful.

2

Basket of
found mushrooms
        like
a pound
or so.
I can
cook them
        up
unless
    they're toxic
in which
case I'll throw them
in the waste
    paper basket.

3

I read Peirce and Whitehead
back to back.
I understand little
but what I do understand
is enough
                          unless
I know less
than
I think
I do

4

More and more
I'm out      of    ideas
                    un-
less
you count
        my fingers.

## TOUCH

Teleology of touch
deferred indefinitely
by drugdreamed dragon rasp,
transmogrified by Time's
elliptical slip such that nothing-
ness unites with nothingness
across the voided chasm,
full and therefore inverted,
that makes touch talk.
We know this
whether we want to or
not, the we we'd be
notwithstanding, the soul
we'd have neversaid, but
there's no question of
knowledge per se
in equations of these proportions
or dimensions, and, as
in dreaming, the distance
between touch and touched
expands. There's an infinity
about it, but it's too much
to think about. Like running
your fingertips along
a shattered window
and seeing your face
in the bloody shards.

# SOUL

The story itself
        is irrelevant
as are the feelings
        it animates.
Trying to find my soul,
I learned only
        of sentences,
long ones, extending
margin to margin or
time to time, found only
the sung song of interrupted
        rupture, sprung form
and split meaning, expression
soul's way out, found what
        I found regardless.
It's the same if I tell it
        twenty-five times,
but only then, otherwise, inevitably
and indubitably, it's different, you see,
the way I remember it
        and the way it really was.
I remember
        trying to find my soul
but finding instead
        a key, osseous and bright,
with which I'd open
        some unknown lock, revealing some
equally unknown but somehow less mysterious

contents. Less mysterious for
lack of soul, for one, but too,
it's true, there are light years between
searching and finding (distance not time,
space not—) but remembering
          too, is irrelevant.
Trying to find my soul,
          I heard music, at first overheard,
          then encountered,
long love spun slowly, music soul's cerement
          in its way, absolute or otherwise,
soul sentenced by music to time, sentenced
by listening to soul's ceremonial presence,
          hearing, through time, becoming
the finding I needed, if not through
          effort or searching. There's
no story there, no memory either.
Soul was never mine, but a sentence
limps to its protractive conclusion,
and, trying to find my soul,
          I flung myself
out of an open window
and landed in a pool of soft fruits,
yellow, slimy, comforting, not
          sickly sweet, but
ripe, and somewhere in there,
          soul, perhaps, but not mine,
never mine. Never mind, it's time,
and, trying to find my soul,

I wrote a sentence I never
wanted to end, and when it ended,
        I called it a story, but
I knew it really wasn't. Trying to find soul,
        I persist, looking out from
behind my eyes to encounter, this time,
the world, where soul gets its meaning from,
        and walk that walk across
who knows what road,
        sliding along as slowly as I please.

## The Occasion

The occasion
it is thought
        cannot foresee
the arborescent structure
of its interior—
                        The hunt is not
                                in itself
                        the condition of an altered
                        mode of mind rot—
fertilized thinking
        growth against tree


It's me under the bolted grate
a clamberer among rats we know
I return now to *its* under
                        side
and won't deride their
        subterranean home—
We speak under speech
derelict barnyard we'd told stories
                of
the cornhusk moon and
                all that
drat there's a rat in there
I know it—

Soapspun antiquities
                    unburdening
          their anterior eaves
          unbearable layering of tomorrows—
and measure for measure
it's all there
          in the original
          occasion

# Abstract Oasis

You have come for what you
do not know. There is air
yet to be breathed, water yet to be
drunk, sinister sisters carrying water
or a baby to a rocky ledge, and you,
defined by Time's seeming limitlessness,
stand for nothing, upright and symbolical as
the ledge itself, speaking your dreams
out loud, telling what only you can
tell.

You have come for relief from all
that there is. What have you to
say for yourself, lone forager among
deceptive stones, looking for one with
just the right coloring, if the light and shadows
allow, to be swallowed whole
by the eye, try as you might, finding
only gray? It is today, but it is also
tomorrow, where your search concludes and
you see.

The ledge is Time. The baby merely
a stone, and the sinister sisters, Satan's
conjugal offspring, hoist with helping hands
memoranda and material belonging. Automaticity
notwithstanding, feeling as you go, soul

travelers bearing the brunt of the burden,
*biological speculation sittin' here vibratin',*
under the tattered auspices of plain saying,
it's only one soul, but separate husks.

*Free your mind and*
*your ass will follow. Find the self*
*and kill it.* The old gods tell
new truths. Candleflame and images
of the dead adorn the sacred space
in mind, you, coming, see death
as a question of mere positioning
within the cosmic landscape or
seascape or dreamscape, escape
the form the dream takes
when you finally arrive.

Bone and feather, tied together, make
marvelous organisms. Life's spring,
even in stone, tells that the ground
beneath sacred feet is not enough
to save those sisters, to save the baby,
all the babies, or to save time.
Desert swordsman hunting
for stones, slicing at cosmic debris, at
lions and baobabs, hears a message
from another world. It is you
who speaks, speaks thus:
Time cannot destroy you, but it
will anyway.

Sacredness and stink, sacrilege
and the beauty of the eternal
dance, all form one image:
A headstone, a skull, mourners
dressed in ceremonial white, one
picture in the mind of Time, bleached
like a bone or an angel of a certain
kind, mind what made death
come alive. Mysterium tremendum. Blood
letting made art, hopping between the streams,
to look the elders in their collective eye.

Standing still, you've saved no one, not
even yourself, but Time, evacuated of meaning,
rolls forward, an empty vessel
soon to be smashed.

## Stop in the Name

If you want to understand poetry
    get over it!
The skin and the sky conspire
    to define
the criteria by which
    we apprehend
over and over
    that mountain
of meaning we're
    standing on,
that we stood under
    since that birth
of ours, some called collective,
    others called
wrong, ripped out from
    non-existence,
thrown toward that
    armagideon we'd
already intuited but never before
    read about, already foretold but
never before gotten over,
    already enslaved, it seemed
we were, standing under
    the overpass, hands over
hungry mouths, held up hailing
    a cab, we waited and
waited, but eventually
    we walked,

made it late for the over
   under, reasoning
with ourselves that Time
   is there for us,
Time's a tide to get caught
   under, somebody said.
If you want to understand Time,
   roll over!
Our reasonings are real,
   heels clacked on
black tar as
   he approached,
and thus we knew,
   aware but not
afraid, we brayed,
   rested on the wrong
day, he said
   he saw us,
   bless up, we said
back, we said black, we said
   creaks so we said
crack, the pressure of expression
   before the face
of the force that
   stops us, faceless
it could be
   if we let it,
standing before

the black horizon,
quick, cool, deadly,
the we of the wind
we found ourselves
riding on
fading into shadow
and I alone
remain, trying to find
what's true,
trying to pray
my way out
regardless of belief
since the swift
wind had all but
stopped and
the psychic debris
of spontaneous separation
lingers longer than
expected, and if
I die here, I'll have died
only in name.
If you want to understand death,
it's only a stop-over!
Big ups on the overpass,
looking erstwhile
east, into the night
bright flight of nether
light, lust upon that

wicked laughter we
heard in our communal
    dream, born of this
moment, of I alone and I
    at home, and perhaps
a third I, mingling
    among the carcasses
of long forgotten
    dead in long forgotten
lands, ritual rebirth predicted,
    rite of death undefined,
but the dream stopped
    under the overpass
and whether by waking
    or by death, we wandered
here and I think we'll
    stay a while.
If you want to stand over
    stop.

## Presentation

After a heavy snow, the silence ensnares contingencies of the moment
and it is only before subsequent rainfall that the sensorium bursts.

An empty light-socket, potential and all, wood and green and sap.
A fetal pig, plucked for devouring, bed and blanket and feather.

I am what you made me and cannot think in
       images.
It's always a matter of truth. Not as in
       civilization or
              disclosing,
not as in machine, but as in organism,
in breath as it carries its droplets of moisture
from life to life, steam to stream
and the careful elongations of a trepidatious truism.
*Al(l) truisms are false.*           But not.
       If useful
       the objects
       are to be
       taken
       to the places
       of their expected
       use.
             *We are the expected use.*
Multivalent valediction, they were violent
       before they left, shoes on wrong
*feet feet feet*, hallelujah! how they walked

like their puppeteer'd had a spasm
o'er and long to that rural chasm
whereupon they'd leapt to their
            elegant snuff and then
just as the moon began to rise
the plum trees pendulating hanging from their roots
I saw them there and
                        for the length of a moment's
                        slipstream
accreted rather than disclosing,
inherited, but critically
and in the vast wake behind the eyes of the experience
saw snowdrifts in someone else's memory.

## TRYING TO TELL THE STORY

Datum of memory: *it was bed's edge we sat on*
                          *feet reached floor*
                          *but hardly*
Significance appears only
after the abutting wall's been
          blown over, not the fourth
but the fifth, between the I and
          the eye—needle it knew'd be
          threaded, need not remember
          to reperceive.
Datum of memory: *hair birthed blood*
                          *birthed skin*
                          *birthed hair*
The poem's in black
and white, as if written
          on a chalkboard
          but not
          quite. White, white,
          the color of clouds
          and sugar, *black as midnight*
          *black as pitch*
          The laughter doesn't carry
          over the wall.
Datum of memory: *a question of selection*
                          *not natural*
                          *but mad*

I don't care to remember
it anymore, but if there is
an I and it must, it would
eliminate the conditional.

*iron away coil*
*lament the inconvenience*
*of birth by other*
*orders*

The data of the memory congeal into nothing.
There is no constellation to glean from its star points.
Only white pinpricks in a night sky, endlessly black.

## The Landscape

The landscape, here,
    is immaculate
    in its way.


        *Immaculately despicable!*
Privacy is privative,
    so say they who live east of here, or west. (*culture, labor, apostle, season, sea*)
and so a life lived here is a life lived as anywhere, anywhere at all.


        *Concrete conceptual detail, the grinding scream of*
        *a forest animal someone told me was a fisher*
        *cat, "It sounds like someone being murdered"*—*the passive is less painful.*
When you've announced yourself
you've announced your demise
as a marble-worker, chipping away
at your own freedom.


        *Concrete emotional detail, profound confusion*
        *at the experience of encountering one's own*
        *countenance, in the mirror, in childhood.*
The difference is clear.
"The person in whose skull the tongue is moving"—

The landscape of the inner world,
   where the anger comes from,
   where the suffering comes from,
inherits its shape from the first spoken words.


    *Not spoken! Heard! The first heard words!*
The passive is less painful.

## First Image

The rockers of a rocking
chair rock the child
in the singing woman's arms,

    charms,
    indelible little things,
    foreclosing the then nascent
    possibility of evading
    their determinacies,

spreading themselves,
between two separate
cycles of inhalation and
ex, two separate
cycles of lub-dubbing
and the flat of the scarred palm
beating itself against
the child's brown back.

    Ransacking
    the memory,
    the placement of its pictures,
    the child, one no longer,
    looks beyond death

and emaciation
to this origin-
ary state of
rocking himself
into existence,
of being rocked into
being, of awakening
in maternal arms.

> I cannot tell you if I'm dreaming
> for I cannot move, only be
> > moved, cannot hurt,
> only be hurt.

## SELF-PORTRAIT

A child discovers art
      when, in school,
a teacher tells him
      to draw his own
                 face.
Fractured and rapacious,
the urge to build
      transmits itself
into the minds of
      children
under varying
      material and moral
circumstances.

"To become a formed being—" which meant
      to form and inform, reform and perform

      *the self in accordance with the rule*
        *of the other*

and darken the image with ink.

The child raises his hand backwards.

      *the political conditions*
      *of light and its aftereffects,*
      *of dreams and their*
      *component parts*

*cannot reveal*
*the child's experience.*

The picture will appear upon the wall
There is no second chance at making self
The mirror, once abstracted, plays its trick
            inside of language,
            its primordial condition
            and existential homecoming,
and offers only ostensibly
an increased quantum of fidelity
to the processes of reality
that bleed out the child's
            drawing.

Flesh colored paper
        they have
        in these
                schools.

The dimensions of the image
        are infinite
like a face inked over
eyes and all.

## Sound's Morning Excess

*A poem is a single word*
*naming a sensual unknown – Robert Kelly*

Listening, the individual
does its divine part, pushing
the stone in its inevitable
direction. It is an activity
done only and never
alone. Vibratory matter encrusts
acoustic wave, gave soul its
generative potential, gives
continually mud its merciless
stick. It's too serious for
metaphor, meaning made across
the dripping mouthhole, of the spaces
between words and objects, filled
perhaps with nothingness, perhaps
with air, perhaps with the invisible
ordering principle by which concepts
affix themselves to experience. Mud's
stick in stone, sticks and stones break
bread before bones, bread before houses,
bread before dusk, darkness settling
in the corners of one's eyes, rise
beasts of the night, the time for flight
is upon you. Wingbeat yields boom
perhaps cosmic, brown stone thrown
down in the mud, where it sticks until
dawn. Individually, you cannot move
it, but its condition is not constant. Sound's

solid form, stones offered to that noble
listener by earth, wretched and blesséd at once,
earth made of mud, made for mud, above all
made, techne the ground of ground, the site
of sight, the thrill of sound. Made mud
the stuff of made dreams, made sound
the source of soul's lifegiving water, these
made things make things awake, in
principle, at a moment's limp notice,
suspended there, in time, in no time,
in sense, in no sense, created
but only in a sense, by the very nature
of sound and of stone. One can't do it,
but two, O divine division, multiply
your lengthening body, and build stones
from thin air, push stones toward their
origins in ear. Bend the marble edifice
and if it shatters, bathe in the jagged pieces,
cut your face and bleed. This is the task
of moving the stone, natural rock carved
but without lasting, the stone will become
dust and even its messages, divine such as they are,
will go mute. Touch the tawny stone, O child,
O owlet, O nightbird beckoning brave spirits
assemble, stone totem trembling when it
senses you. Your touch enables light,
birth, morning. The sky unhinges its
terrible jaw, the throat of the universe
inhales with all its force, the original individual
shattered, stone dust all that's left.

## OUTSIDE THE GILDED WINDOW

Outside the gilded window
demons have taken to the streets.
In single file, they march and
chant and stomp. I know they are
demons, for I can see their faces
contorting in the light of the dying
sun, changing as only a demon's
can. Faith, it is written, is the substance
of things unseen, seeing sound made
substance, sound heard as faith's terrestrial
harbinger. Can those demons hear
the sounds their stomping feet make? Do
they know where they are going? Yes
is the answer that avails itself, truth
notwithstanding. Yes, the window,
whose golden hinges squeak with
age, opens unto their streetside
rage but, closed or open, I cannot
see through the glass. Yes, I hear
the demons scream, as though inviting
me downward to join. I know not
what they march for, nor how their
feet connect to their legs. I know nothing
of their origin either, ignorance's withering
tackle the original onset of fear, Time's
coy announcement, life's flimsy foundation.
But I know they're demons, the shifting faces
trading places in amongst their rank
all the proof I need. A book on the shelf
begins to glow. Unassuming spine begets

unknown name, mystic light begets

unassuming attention, assumed there all

the same, lusted after all the while, defiled

by the unread years, it's clear why it's

glowing but I cannot say. Spinal bareness,

in the light of the gilded window, dusk approaching

rapidly as the sun continues its daily descent, reminds

of scripture, of textual ecstasy amounting to God, of

dead things rendered live by mere inertia. What

chants I can hear are not in words, but

conjure the image of the Book no less. Whence

this strange light, the sun, the moon, the aching

stars, the Book of all books, the final sound

before the rapture? Demons never betray

their truer motives. The sky is turning

purple. Trees crackle in hellish blaze. I

am drawn to the window because

I lack a stable sense of self, because

my psychic constitution emerged

as if from nowhere. This, the this

only the demons know, is merely

a feeling. I was born in this

moment, built of this particular light, this

particular air, formed in the sonic slipstream

made by the chants and stomps outside

the window. I recede. The window is

there and the demons, now moving faster, movement's

pulse persisting amidst even mystical conditions, have

taken on a new color. Gold, the moon just rising, refracts,

experience interrupts language's natural music,

the Book opens itself and the demons laugh, not

because the Book is funny, but because demons

are playful by nature. Kaleidoscope sky, unstable
ground, horizon stripped and slipped along
circular surface, the remaining eye, that cavity
initial demonic assessment flowed from. There is
nothing out there, no sky, though its colors
change, no trees, but still they burn, and no
demons, whose march, quickening, quickening,
advances along as entropy, beyond the sound
it all makes. The pages of the Book turn
on their own. Bursting soul, incandescent Heaven,
religion in the palms, demons in the street, straight
down the path insisted on by resistance, least of all
encoded in the Original Book. The music cares
not who hears it, but the soul it emits matters much.
Interruption and rupture coextend, self's recession
portended by demonic invitation, initiation a matter
of listening, listening a matter of soul—the repetitions
evince the consistency of the path, chosen under
mystical conditions, self effaced at just the right
time. Color among color, the sky has become
black. The fires, purifying in their way, persist.
The book has burst into flames. It is fair. It is fair.
We have risen. We will march. Its words, divine
like the light at the center of soul, beckon us
run. The music we make the haunting initiation
  of night.

## On Composing

Elected legibility whispered its way
       in, tore open my head with
its sound. Thought I'd lost it, just
       adrift on a cognitive sea,
rafted and thereby afloat, throat churning
       draft made real by elected legibility's
elected remembrance. Censured sound made
       sense under duress of expression,
expressiveness missed its mixed expanse
       even so, so there I was, elected legibility's
whiff still with me, mixed grip what it took to hold
       on to all the same. Legibility's
swift election left sameness out in the same rain,
       soaking in the sense its sound made,
tearing open my wet head again, and then it was
       then that elected respite's originary force
yielded legibility after all. Elected respite's primacy,
       that shadow-wanting in the guise of ease,
allowing for election after the fact, is what makes
       things legible, in certain states, states of
certainty, of grace, of matter, of affairs,
       of stained-glass glistening in an old
god's gift, blasted and lambasted in the same sun
       of its dizzying image, whose clandestine erasures
obscure real heat, elected respite prayer's way out
       nonetheless. In my head, the ringing bell
signals a turn to stewardship, to patience, to attention,
       to elected legibility's parental listening, to elected
respite's provisional rest, addressed to myself, I speak
       by listening, to express only as in to squeeze,

election and legibility, ancestral gifts, cosmic and magical,
coming only when called for, called for only
at dawn. State's election, its double-sensed power, elected
by election's strict reluctance, recalcitrant though it appeared,
elected respite notwithstanding, violence awaiting dialectical
rupture, state awaiting dialectical rupture
more than once, the sense I mean lost, sound sending sorrows
across delicate and gentle Time, whose mythic transgress
enacts dogma in the technical sense, lies, contravenes myth,
synonymous though they seem, by bearing the weight of its
unexamined beauty, its innocent or naïve light, its daffodils
behind the chirping, a chickadee stuck in an open carcass,
parakeet beauty, owlet regress, sunder by wingbeat, hawk, vulture, sparrow,
elected legibility programmed by category, Aristotle
notwithstanding. Legibility and state, shoulder to
shoulder on the same ledge, function their dialectical dependent,
noun or verb all the same, appendage stapled to bloody
nub, twilit river a destination worth running to,
speak their unity by the cuts they've
riven, sustained, borne, torn at the seam, torn
musculature as collateral meat, peatmoss dredge against
muck and slime of the aching bones that amount
to the skeleton I'm sitting in, elected legibility's reluctant receptacle.
I am here.
It is where I am.
There is nothing to be found beneath
the ground I lay down daily, nothing
to be seen beyond the limits of daylight's frame. I cannot go
where I am not led. The seasons proceed. The mind
drifts. Elected legibility's residual tint
calls back, sonic dreamscape from which only
resistant escapes are possible. I proceed.

Each brick lain, each sound listened to, soul's wicked whisper, fructifying and healing. I am here.

It is light.

The sea makes its tidal mark upon the skeletal shore, organs packed up tight. There is a destruction in it. A loss. A death. A void.

And I believe, true or false, that I too am a bird.

Electing legibility all the same.

## MEDITATION

Laryngitic, descending the stair
     from whence those blessings arrived
and bled them with their selfish stare, the brimming
     cookpot rusted out by hatred's abiding fire
given life by the grace of the almighty stare, hung judges
     by ignition's righteous supply, given hinges, given
surge, poisoned provisional access accosted distracted vision,
     programmed metaphorical freedom, taken by the token,
elicited limitation on the igneous bridge, its ridge abiding light
     and portion provided thus. Barren, its vast haunches rising
in the dying light, trembling with sound, cultivating vision via
     virtue derived ground—sound, sense, sensorium purporting
love, purporting life well-lived, purporting solidarity—envisioning
     light. Do not follow. Envision only yourself at the water's
rough edge, seaspray sunlight tithing warmth to your aching
     temples, tips touching only form them, amended mourning
of sunshine's crystal whip, faking it in the face of terrestrial
     explanations. Planetary enrollment given fool, given fuss, given
ephemeral stare, given something to hold onto, a payoff no less, no
     less tested, no less known, unknown beholder of Time's aching
eye, its lagging abrasiveness abreast of rested love. Simplicity's rhythmical
     abandon, clarity's abiding thud, *give em something to hold onto*, hold
only your temples, concussed, rusted like a cookpot of forgotten use
     value, dusted over by dead skin and snow. I heard it, not
in a dream, but in that third state, the one you wait for like a watched
     pot, never coming, never coming, never Time's suspended sentence,
coming its ineluctable limit, arrival never's unbecoming, and thus
     it arrived and I became, connecting the inner and outer
eyes, I's eye an I worth finding, not a me, not a man, not even a mouse, but
     a voice, broken and hoarse, blessings of sound and sense, sentience

no less identified, mind no less summoned. It isn't really
        a voice. It is a dream voice, language made flesh by non-vocal
mechanica, voice given flesh by simple means, simpler than meaning, simpler
        than Time, simpler than the synapses that govern these pointless
forays, simpler than a child birthed then clothed, dying as an old woman, naked
        and alone. The husk hardens. The I grows slack. It's only a game
for those who haven't done the listening, phlegm filled falsetto foretelling slow
        movement, prophetic abundance in meditative ease, please, don't wait for me,
I'll take my Time. Where did it come from, I once was tempted
        to ask in the darkness, but when no answer came, when no one could
help me, I found I's question lacking, confused. It was when, not where, in a different
        Time both old and new, sound's primordial source an inverted echo
heard from the bottom of that unknown stair, the stair it's already descended, no sounds
        to hide behind, Time's residual behind blown back by the listening
we must do. Must, doing's hidden infringement, chained to its own signifying,
        to get only as far as we want to go. I've heard it once. I've heard it
again. Might as well have heard it a thousand times. But the matter
        at hand breeds apocrypha, breeds matter, breeds noble
truths. I can endure neither noise nor silence. Almighty speech
        a blessing in bodily disguise. It lies. It lies. But it doesn't
matter. There is no searching, no waiting, no finding—only
        eternal arrival, foretold but not predicted, and directionless
movement among the slugs.

## THE SHOUT AND THE POLIS

*Drown the dogs first*
an angel replied to a citizen
 of the Republic of First Deaths
and Ignoble Births. The art
of asking isn't a question
of truth, but of drowned dogs,
bloated and waterlogged, who'd
died as they'd been born, mute
but for the squealing, pain but
for the healing, and the undulating
muscle beneath tense, taut skin,
taught sin by self from the bookshelf
of the damned, embalmed and enflamed
and bespoiled by Time whose righteous
directedness impels mourning.
*The onion sun sets before our waking eyes.*
A citizen or a subject is constituted
by the Republic in which it dwells
in the abstract. The politics
is in the making. Polysemous plinth,
parallel portico, colonizing colonnade,
it is a built thing we've encountered,
made of words and time and blood,
as all things are at the right conceptual
level. There's dust on the insides
of my eyelids and Time knows no
witness to the drives one abides
in the snowbank night, cathecting
oneself to unexpected entry and
*received modes.* The I whose lids

are on the table couldn't summon
an angel. Nor is vision a possibility
beyond the putative powers of
waking, the omnipresent clock-ticks
and shock-tricks of linearity
rising thru sleep to attest to the nether-
world's unctuous aftereffects.
*The snow is blinding here.*
Dogs dream, selflessly, of unboundedness
and the chase.

# It

It's the same,
man, what you
say when you
see that it's
me on
　　　the
page in
　　　the
dream of
　　　the
screen and
　　　the
scream of
　　　the
　　　　　　*aereopostephocitis*
of the lungs
and the spleen
so I seem
to be seen
as a man
or a black
or a fog
or a dream
or a da.
No more words.
Just sounds. Make
no signs for
me or you
for we and
they for on

and on post-
world word faced
by now, thru
you made sound
and song, death
by time's real
crunch on lungs
of beasts who
drive on wrong
roads out land.
Fuck the count.
We dreamed
      the wrong stage.
We burned
      the wrong dream.
*Dance Dance Dance*
It waits there.
It's cash, dog,
all played out,
laid out back
by the shed
and the post
dance whip lick
scar, skin, skein
we mean by
beat, but not
      by blood.

## First Plea

*Damn all the possibilities*
            *you raise*
*by abandoning your body*
            *for the social*
*praise*
                        *and talking*
            *the fermented reek*
*of performance.*

Speech is a dead
                        giveaway
for that act
            the voice
                        named. The voice,
utterer of I, the commander-God
of language, speaks into being
a fear of separation
between body
and self and tells in speech that
            the act is vicious,
            dishonest,
            malignant,
and that to be seen is always
already to perform.

*Expression of desire*
            *or lack*

Raising in the sun
the expression displays
itself    *for consumption*
and amidst that castle black
sea of heads and eyes
casting their gazes back
onto the commander-God
who sunders self from
self under the sign of its
own aleatory power.

A child asks for his life back.
The universe hums.

## MOUNTAIN PEAK DREAM

In the face
       of
            it

all
       we bend the
knee
       and try
to wash
       what we
           can.

There it is!
In the dreamspace!
Just there, beyond that peak!
We hardly climb,
but clamber, you and me. Too,
the space of it—*the space of it!*
Personal decay metastasizes in
side of the human      subject
but we can see it
all the more clearly
from up      here.
*Do you feel it?*
You breathe the question
and, stung up by cold
air, lungs expand and
contract inside you.

Pinch, in between your
black    fingers the snow.
*Do you feel it?*
The question from elsewhere
black    n blue, cracked
up on a winter Sunday (never said
cracker on the mountain top)
never said nomad, nonsensical
conquest, the wind in the
question as                breathed.
Never said breath on this never
said mountain top, the dreamspace
sputters, loses light like
losing lucidity, losing
breath and never said
speech. *Do you feel it?*
The question, rendered
hollow, echoes through these
mountains. And the never said
birds sing their never said song.
On and on.
                Exhale.

## I MEAN HERE

I mean here.
We[1] speak of things I would not dare repeat
for fear of putting you[2] to listless sleep.
Here, there, and especially there, the natural[3] evades our[4]
attempts at holding it down.

I mean here.
No saying[5] where, where a dog[6] sniff's another's
anus[7], where a man[8] collapses to his aching
knees and calls out to his god[9] in prayer, where the reverse[10]
could never[11] not be untrue too.

I mean here.

---

1  Not you and I, but rather those whose habits of mind carve their limits into the public stone.

2  Waking, breathing, secreting, desiring, consuming, omitting, aborting, perspiring, perusing, combatting, dreaming, dreaming, dreaming.

3  Natural speech, the natural rhythms of the natural heartbeat, the natural domination of the natural weak, the natural work of the natural week, the natural day, the natural sun setting in the natural sky, along the natural horizon seen from behind the natural eyes of the natural subject, the natural language of a natural poem.

4  We the people, think particular, we the people, non-curricular, we the people, *the only dish of peaches in the world, these, these, these.*

5  The tongue as much the diaphragm, the mind as much the organ.

6  The ear, the eye, a flash, quickslip of the species whereby, they say, to walk is joy.

7  Orificial question, nutritional extraction, existential option.

8  Not a dog.

9  Neither dog nor man.

10  Rising in reverse, rising as the tide, rising as the moon, rising, a white sheet shown to be blown by the wind, she rose and rested in the same shawl.

11  You've gone wrong. There are no things in themselves. *The beginning and the end co-constitute the middle* we said with silence on either side of it.

In multiple[12] deaths and surviving origins[13], in substituting
one word[14] for another, one letter for a fingernail, in just
making it from waking to sleeping, in speaking[15]
on the telephone with a stranger[16] about my internet provider.

---

12   The primary substance (sub-linguistic problem of stance)

13   Already critiqued, awaiting material destiny.

14   And in the beginning

15   Light

16   I mean here

## LAKE EFFECT

The blue-black face
from that unknown
            place
returns its gaze
from the sea-foam green
surface of the lake.
I reject the idea
of description but
            embrace
category and name.
Aquamarine,
with its crack and crescendo,
beginning with mouth open,
ending with tongue on teeth,
is itself a name
that description
constitutes.
Color never describes.
You cannot describe
a grain of sand
but you can name one,
name them all,
and in those names you
will find a
            trace
of the flame-flicker soul
of the objects an observer
differentiates.

(who can't swim) shine
(dig) shoes for nickels, which,
like grains of sand,
have scarcely discrete identities.
The face appears again,
now between my legs on the surface,
and with my feet I dig the sand
to create a hole, an empty
       space.
The face remains
       my face.
The sky is purple.
A boat floats.
Purple is the sky.
And, in their
       place,
the stars emerge,
as if from nowhere.

## STONE

In only a stone's throw,
      small stone on wet hand,
*Act!*—two birds, you know the rest.
The it is in the doing, if you understand
 the stone, but I
never have and, even if I live
long enough, prolly never will.
Clean the dirt from the stone
with lakewater. Washing its
surface will wash, too, the world
of its putrid violences, mislaid claims
and practical consequences, exegetical
excesses and errant imaginings, manticores
and such,
      the demented detritus of incorrigible
dreamstates, and tropical storms somewhere
near the equator—would you rid
    the stone
        of these?
Stones are often dirty
    in the world,
especially this one
        here,
where the ancients prophesized we'd be,
and the anarchic purity of the celestial body
runs its wrinkled fingers down the spine of Time,
carving snowflake shaped scars into Time's
ostensibly immortal backflesh

blackflesh, the gap between word
and world, the gap between these
united bodily states
of interminable stasis, anti-
vital, inorganic state apparatus
of break, slipped elliptical
vision of atrocity , cylindrical market
I'm told of, *dirty money, ain't it funny*—
the wrinkled hand turns and the stone
slides off and back into the water.
The hand will return to its original condition.
The stone will sink to the lake's earthen floor.

## ON DIFFICULTY

It's difficult
man     keeping it
real     against those
occlusions of lifting the heavy
tome off the top shelf        stepladder
slip all too probable for some.
The pub in public shifting
gears from its evident estrangement
in whose image we demand clarity
but it isn't the difficulty
that's the problem. It all happens
much sooner     before over becomes
under     before the scatter backed daftness
eclipses spiritual fluorescence and
the intervening paralysis extends beyond its
first encounter. Real      bad adverbs lipping
the heavy split it emits     real's last time
portending doomed particulars
the myth of *hidden signification* begets
a closed-book lexicon        difficulties
communicating     particular facts
in certain contexts       erudition
notwithstanding. A function
of class seen only from the outside       inside
spirit book fused and thus learnèd        binding
and blinding class       as is its function
materiality irrelevant all the same.
Let me bathe myself
in the toxic sludge       in righteous praise

of the *there* of words      in giving thanks

for the heavy tome's nectar. Difficulty

precedes me      proceeds from me

under      malevolent care I've been

difficult      hostile architecture of burdensome

soul      felt presence of *linguistic complexity*

made not of money but of soul's internal

rumble      the *therefore* what's suspect      so

let the dogs out and let them dig

until they find what they're looking for

then you'll know      how to hear

the dense musicality of soul's

endemic sputter      pulse hinged

sustaining and enlightening      cookpot

rhythms deeper than the eyes go      limp

like a leper at a certain time      to find

what was there all along. You've heard it

and it's there and the high shelf lowers

and the tome is there

but it will only help you

so much.      There's a world

between *A* and *Z*. Busting down

the doors      we've assembled your meanings

but deny the accusation. I'm tired. Record scratch

refraction begets soul's ceremonial upset      gesture

of moonlight and fading plumes of smoke.      Terrestrial

bodies withstand cosmic motion      the densest

musicality      all that's left.

## Dialogue with Acclivity

*Diaphanous daffodils for sale at a sundries stand*
*unarmed widget offers unanimous forensic implication*
*and an officer of the law concocts*
*some mammal with a prehensile tail*

Thematic material, inveterate invertebrate,
I think in terms already devised for me,
not quite shared but
       mutually imposed,
as if imposition and implication,
impish hidden heart of language,
together render limp the possibility
of transcending limits—
       it's all its own thing
           now,
now that the necessary temporal conditions
have been sufficiently met and
now that definitions have been
all but obliterated and
now that analysis, abandoned with alacrity,
has measured itself against finitude,
*Now now* she says in the abstract,
not the empty musings of a would-be mystic
but the would-be musics of a composite
organism, its face, its shoes, its terrible
tendons, the should-be mystics of a should-be
Zion, babylonian bombsquad been suffered thru,
financial machinery not so different,

                    different contradiction
I'm told—


*At the appropriate pace, even*
*stasis moves*
*diaphanous daffodils and other*
*such material things*
*from one space to*
*the next*
            *ad infinitum*
*until the axial core of*
*terrestrial experience*
*encircles the objects it aims to explore*
*culminating in a feather-tailed mammal,*
*a steel-toed boot and iron bars,*
*ripe lemons and political teeth,*
*tooth on top of tooth, body on top of*
*body, land on top of land—*
                                    *this side of it, I see it as it is*

## THE REAL THING

There's an outside
     real,
slung gun in the hot sun
     and an inside
real,
     heart of the lunar
movement of thinking
     while writing
while dreaming
     while shitting,
while playing an assailing wail
     of screeches
     on the jukebox
of the interior—superior conquest
conquistador no doubt.

The unraveling of one
is the ultimately constitutive property
of the other and
therefore, its originary source,
its murky womb and elegant
tomb, deciduous bomb
blown back by.
*By abiding the one we forsake the other.*

It never pays to think in puzzles
       but words lose their currency
in the liberal bazaar,
         and it seems
that all of the unraveling
         is for nothing.

It is here that the two sorts of real merge, where the poem combusts,
where the sunset eyes of Time enlighten and corrupt and betray and
nourish, and the architects of misery
      take off their own heads.

## Once Around the World

Lateral longing
      belonging to
the bellows and red dead
bedfellows, who cast their lot
in stones—it's the matrixial stitch,
      the solstice of most
blessed rejoinder to the void's
      repeated insistence
on abandon and quick, a second's
long awaited elliptical split in which
      spun rubber begets
material satisfaction. It's all in it,
this business, what's cut from colored
      cloth, what cuts the cost of ill-gotten
grains, fed and feasted all at once, and thus divine,
divined our time in the same stones, bones a man
danced for there on the floor, sustained game of tapping
and waiting, charting severed seasons across aborted familial
      answers, answers, ancestors, cancer,
 rust riven parapet of soul and soul's
sustaining grain. It feeds, one feasts, but it's not
the same, remaining to be seen what it says
      nonetheless and all the same,
erstwhile irking ephemeral legalities, consulting
prodigious voracity on the physical plane, its birth
      assembling life before our naked, naked
eyes, the disguise of novelty preparing us for
      achieving consciousness
after a long and treacherous slumber, counting stars
as quarters amidst an economy of light, participatory

endorsement in numbers, numeral split

      across paid time's slip, numerology notwithstanding,

faith's embrace of reckless erasure

      what was longed for, even beyond its apparent

possibility. The birth is long, creation's agon its own medicinal

      whiff, flipped switch on existence edging out prenatal

sleep, descending, descending, erupting, transcending,

      transforming the conditions of one's surround, once

around the world and it's back to bed, dead letters enlivening

      dirty cloth strips, the work itself changing, the work itself

changed, dirty strips of cloth stripped of color, synesthetic aesthetic

      bearing down the sound of it, intrinsic enigma

and ineluctable surface casting conspiratorial glances, chance made actual,

      wish made real, wheel turned on the axis of its eventual

invention, madness made text, sound made sense, birth made

      vengeful, man's made money, second skin

what it's in till its end. It isn't about anything

      given its pleasure principle and neuroplastic

tendencies, elongating at the frame for a finite

      length, sliding abominably backward at

the bending spine, defined and limited by time's

      inhibiting grip, inertia's reversals engendering

character on the scale of psychoanalysis, character

      that refracts its action across a cosmic instant

of accordianlike visions, waking only descriptively, and thereby

      infinite, but only if one listens. The longing of the gotten

grain, itself attending the possibilities of creation inside its own

      subjectivity, mind, mind, experience, design,

the ending predicted by the preceding event, the ending eventual

      and original all the same. Bad, bad music

plays softly in wax-filled ears, ringing out to release itself

      into the bad, bad mind, where legibility's ledge

edges its way inward and, teetering along it, legs broken and bleeding,
  *legere, legere, ka, abara, legere*
Latin and Yoruba consigning appropriated value to the activity
  of extracting, enigmatic avoidance and cryptographic ice
chill the soul fires lit in bad music's lighting, campfires of residual
  meaning flickering in soul's solar wind heat, and just like that,
meaning leapt, the chasm beneath it nonetheless there,
  empty, persisting, eternal, blank,
and it's only as one tumbles
  that one knows it's there.
  Waiting. Waiting. Silence.

## Historical Encounter in False Fugue

False entries of the subject,
voiceless whisper of
> *beasts*
> *birds*
> *fishes*
> *man*

(reason, teacher, ruler)
>> death of the spirit,

I've heard it called. Whisper like a
*wasp* of a certain sort, American obsession
with revolution, English lit
>> up like lamps

lit for a lightshow, little by little, history
accretes, imagination dons diamond-dusted
underwear, the auditory layering of premonitory
voices folds, accordionlike, as
>> history,

and, in accreting, makes music, accordionlike.


Imitation! Imitation! Aspire to the conditions
> of music or, choose your team,
the grinding gear and the beating heart,
> they're images, after
>> all,

and liberate the book from the
book, that leviathan battling its way
through the centuries, and for whom? for
what? the ancients ask, the moderns reflect, and
we, we, (consent of the governed, and so

forth) sit on our thumbs, the false politics
of subject-
      ive material consciousness (death's
relentless approach n
                    all that)

and the voices continue their
terrible speech, political and otherwise,
for as long as our
      ears can bear it.
permutation, transpositional force from
one to one, the sound
      the scream
           O True Leveller Release

## A LOGICAL POEM

If only I knew what was
      what
I'd have a sense
of all that
      is.
Touch me two more times
and see the distance between
      mind and
matter
      it does not
close
      it does not
signify
      it tries.


Do you remember,
      in *Company*,
          the Beckett
      of my
          most unironic love,
when "You are on your back in the dark,"
      the feeling?
      "Yes I remember."
      "Quick leave him."
The common
      place
          book

leaves itself
      carelessly open
on the coffee table,
      where guests can flip through it
      if they are serious.


I never mind
      my
Ps and Qs
      whose
contents, scruted and effed,
are transparent—light
      passes straight through
      illuminating nothing
      enlightening no one.
Still, I find that
      being
      still
makes it all worth
        while.


Repeat yourself for me, dear love.
Semantically take me nowhere.
Repeat yourself—it never ends.
For me, be free, be open.

Lost the feeling in my
    feet
        now.
Lost and found
    what once
        was.
Found the feeling of loss
    like
finding again
    what was
long gone.
Found the feeling in
    our
        feet
    we said,
but we lied
    a
lot.
Whose feet are these, attached to my legs?


If P then Q
P
Therefore—what?
Give me back
    the feeling.

## YOU'RE A NATURAL

Stuttering, the natural
asserts itself in various
          unexpected circumstances,
replicating dreaming so as not
          to take advantage, judging
by the *nat* of it, of Time's way
          of giving things value.
Naturally, the elements involved
          shimmer, refract, emit
and the thing we call
          surprise itself
          is elemental evidence of
elliptical atrocity, speaking back
from that which looks like a dream
but only isn't in accordance with
          certain laws. All natural
feed on this side of the street, eating
with our feet to keep from falling
          in the bowl. A whole dream
transpires between
          two breaths and nature
plays its part, like a mothering animal
          wounded in a war
the mixedness of metaphor
giving way to the real
          textures of violence
dreamed only
          in a sense,

elementally composed though
they are. The natural elements of dreams
      are violent, brought into the world
by force, that war in which the mothering
animal weeps or wept, as you like, born
of the ripping out or ripping up
      of slipped papyrus the sleep spell
was written on, broken speech rendered visible
on decrepit sheet, bleat like the beasts the sheet
made real, made
      naturally from imagined
parts, elements shorn from unknown shores
on which children, familiar but also
      strangely alien, play games as
children do. It's only natural
      you'd see them there, from
across the water, that natural deadness
surrounding you, filling you, enabling
thought and breath and text
      and soul, whatever it is,
even nothing. And as you watch them
or dream them, the mothering animal
      remains audible to you,
even without your straining to hear,
and the crashing waves, a natural symphony,
or silence finally arrived at,
after a long struggle.

## What Do I Do This For? (Ars Poetica)

What do I do this for?
Is it to capture the snow in a cup,
to venerate materiality, melting,
the transitory nature of the shifting
        states we move thru
        or the cold itself?
Is it to excrete as a natural
organism or, as an excreting being,
a being machine, to enact
        repeatedly, the conditions
        of my own
            repeated excretions?
Is it to exonerate form, to enact
via letters or speech some visuo-
material contraption one might
        enjoy with
            coffee and oranges? (*ahhh Sunday!*)
Is it, even, to push the language
        beyond its technocratized
ordinary function, the machinations of capital
        and thus?
Is it to make something happen?
A thousand times no!
I (I) shan't afford the question
        the dignity of coherence and
I (I) stretching out my tentacles
        to touch them to my
        temples

I (I) speak neither in reasons nor in
    pictures but in
        words and
I (I) mean only in accordance with
    that which I'm
        constituted by, that
I (I) surrender before the altar of
    that which
        means and
    that which
        bleeds and
    that which
        screams and
I (I) attack on faith
    the principles of
        construction
    by which one navigates
        oneself and
I (I) imagine a duck taking
    flight over a
    scene of one man ripping
    another man's
    eyes
        out and
I (I) see clearly to the conditions
    that precede all
    others and
        consider it

not at all special
            but essential and
      necessary and
I (I) wasn't born this way
      or that but
      was never an existentialist
      either and
I (I) am interested in
      spontaneous conjunction
      but not
      deterministically,
I (I) believing in nothing
      except for
      *this* and
I (I) appearing nowhere
      except for
      *here* and
I (I) spotted three women placing an infant in a bassinet in a rocky field
beneath a cryptographic sky, the same beneath which three wolves,
black, black, black, one with lustrous silver chest, one with only one eye,
slink in unison, their gigantic paws eerily undetectable to a listener, any
listener, the infant, the women, you, me, I (I), Time, snow, reasons and
the like, the posers of apocryphal queries with impossible conceits, and
the pulsating heart of nothing
      squirting blood for the dead.

## ABSTRACT AUTOBIOGRAPHY

The object, for once, is concrete—
      it's me in there, that thing screaming,
trying to stay alive on fire, melting metal searing
      flesh, body of bodies, mind of
individuated inwardness. The me in the we is trepidatious,
      individuality's residual splat, illusion
I've been told of, nonetheless experienced, here,
      therein, that thing I'm in, that thing
I am, the thing inside the thing—I have no more bones
      to pick, no more stones to throw
down, around the mind's sharper angles, thrown
      into illusion's slipped grip. It's all there,
inside that thing, screaming it's head off, sucking
      dew drops as morning routine,
routinized mourning, farewell to life-death, farewell to
      dew, drinking mourning's morning after, sunset
lullaby on a shoestring's breadth, breath of the self
      in the body of the community, and therefore
I am what it makes me. The me in the we is
      a child, ill-equipped to palm the ground
with enough force to force a kick, to flip or fly or
      flow, floor's resistance to the insistence
of my rough and cracking palms, resistance repeating
      on the edge of the child's personal cliff, the one
he'd fall off just for the thrill, when will eclipsed
      will in the starlight, and the thing inside,
the me inside, bled for a while before it died
      and I left myself, bloody and alone,

waiting. I'm trying to do the thing—
　　　to confess, and that means
the me and the we trading places, speaking from
　　　locations heretofore untold of, unconquered,
internal regions vaster than the vastest sea, vaster even
　　　than that eternal we, the we the me's made up of,
and turn the double inside out, out there in the public
　　　ear, sphere of self, geometric dimension, temporal
suspensions, unrepentant spirit of malevolent self's soul,
　　　giving up the secrets separating the outer and
the inner, whatever their contents, for the other we, the outside
　　　we we read about, the we we'd one day wish we knew,
wish we'd seen among the stars that shone upon our births,
　　　wish we knew in all senses, wish we'd adored
with religious devotion, wish we'd given ourselves over
　　　to. It is in lieu of wish fulfillment that
the inner thing begets the outer, becomes the outer, that thing
　　　inside the thing amounting ultimately
to nothing—because
　　　nothing begets nothing in fleshly situations
and I, conscious of the I inside the I, the I whose I
　　　is divine, tell myself that the me and
the we are finally one, unified by sacredness—but
　　　the thing inside the thing keeps
breathing, the love it lives for, burning, righteousness
　　　at the ready, ready for warfare, ready for
cosmic cadence and ritual abandon, ready for love,
　　　ready for sun ripened fruit eaten before the I

of a real God, beheld for its embodiment in living
      persons and animals. I live in this fantasy,
real as anything, and the thing I am inside me
      burns nowhere but forward,
      loves nowhere but forward,
      and is nowhere but there.
It is a destination I cannot travel to.
The answer, instead, is to drift.

## Morning's Late Return

The sense sets in in
        the morning.

In the interest of time, the light proceeds
across the waking eyelid, conical dustcloud
visible only intermittently, remittance of dream
paid in sleep's ethereal testimony, paid back
slack of night's eradicative darkness, economic
dread what's said in bed before dawn. Earned.

In the sand, life teems. Dustclouds of now's
infinitesimal spread, the only thing we never
grasp, the only thing there is. Peel back opacity,
rise to interior surface, hear, as if for the first time,
the quality of ambient vibratory blank, hot
and wet on the inside, died, bed ridden hidden supply
of dimes from time's effervescent coffers.

       It's cold.        Elasticity elided transpositional
erotics of entertainment, payment on the back burner, fat
burners and elemental
        alterity. It's been said
            that once you're dead
            the violins finally stop
but alas, we go fast as gas this side
        of time's riven roughness,
               where an unbidden past summons

trilobites and sulfur, yesterday's shit, yesterday's
          newspaper, tomorrow's a crowd, two
out of three ain't fallin' for it.


          The usual dryness.      It's time. Motion's
onset, tightness of the chest, meaning's first grimace,
daily awakening's arbitrary symbology, meaning made
          under duress of dream, manufacture what's
at stake in surrendering to that quasi-slip, shockwave shimmer,
frequent trips to Ethiopia or Peru, Babylon or Mars, Purgatory or
deep interior,
the eye hides plainly
          behind the librarian's filthy glasses, legibility on
the table, surface encrusted in dead skin, *it's sin*
          *to see with eyes*
          *that weren't made for ya*
he joked, memory's mystic rift, caustic whiff of old fingers,
          old sweat, old dustclouds of epistemic certainty
enabling early onset cultural maligna, enabling transmission
of soul, the essential paradox, deeper than Zeno or Russell,
          faster still than deriving dream meanings, which
takes time
          by the hand
                    and leads it.
It is a sacred gift we are given. Soul wakes
          alongside time, which guides and elides
dead meanings. It's funny

that thing about morning and mourning. Language, in that
sense, not sight but in the sense of English, of language versus
     *particular languages* such as English, ennobles and prohibits
thought at once, in that heavy state, stated by the poet's god as
     dream, by dream as fear, by fear as
     death, heading toward redness and thunder, heartbeat
and breath, figurative birth or *eternal return*, pleasure
cascades across the waking body, since time's a contradiction
     at root.
First I blink. Second I blink.
     I. I.
     Blink. Blink.
The light requires adjustment. Everything
requires adjustment, the librarian's filthy
     glasses, *economic factors,* the magician's faulty wiring, fake magicians
make real magic, real magicians
     take the light into their wretched bodies and
     cavort in the heavens, dance in that ethereal skylight
as the ground beneath the atmosphere and air turns, turns immaculately,
impossibly, but if you reach down too far, magician I daily address,
magician's eye dresses time by work of magic offerings, offered humbly,
     you'll scrape and bruise your hands,
     as the goings on progress and the light, brightening in one
sense, dimming in another, burns through and across
     the body, worked and expanded, scarred
and kissed and lived,
and died
and burned. Urned.

DEVEN PHILBRICK is a poet and critic living in Ann Arbor, Michigan. He holds an MFA in creative writing from the University of Washington - Seattle and is currently a doctoral candidate at the University of Michigan, where he is working on a dissertation concerning 20th century innovative poetry and process philosophy. He lives with his wife and their several animals.